Making Concrete

Written by Sarah O'Neil
Photography by Michael Curtain

sundance

Have you ever seen
a truck like this?

This is a concrete truck.
It is used to make concrete.

Concrete can be made into
many shapes.
All of these things were made
with concrete.

rocks

cement

sand

Concrete is made from
sand
cement
water
and sometimes rocks.

Concrete made with sand, cement, and water is smooth.

Concrete made with rocks, sand, cement, and water is lumpy.

7

Sam is making smooth concrete.

It is good for sticking bricks together.

This wall is made
of concrete blocks.
Smooth concrete holds
the blocks together.

Lisa is making lumpy concrete.
It is not good for sticking bricks
together.

But it is very strong.
It can hold three bricks.

Heavy trains cross this bridge.
The bridge is made of strong concrete.

This tower is concrete, too!
What other things can be made
with concrete?